Leaked From My Pen Presents

UNCOVERED

Through Christ

MEMOIR SERIES

Book One

Childhood Scars

BY: DELISA TRESHELLE

Published by: Leaked from My Pen, LLC
www.delisatreshelle.com/lfmp

Text & Interior Design by: DeLisa Treshelle
Full Cover Design by: DeLisa Treshelle

ISBN 13: 9781549683589 (Paperback)
10 9 8 7 6 5 4 3 2 1

Scriptures are taken from the NIV (New International Version) unless otherwise notated. Public Domain.

Table of Contents

DeLisa T Writes
@delisatreshelle

if you aren't following the path God created for you. You're hiding and running. That ain't living. God has that life for you but it won't come from you faking it to make it. Don't just look the part. BE the part. And being the part will only come after healing.

Dedication

I dedicate this book to anyone with unhealed wounds. Take some time and get to know yourself. Upon reflection, ask yourself these two questions:

1. *What is at the root of my despair?*

2. *What things are triggering for me?*

Healing is on the other side of revealing those wounds. My prayer is that you will find joy on the other side.

Psalm 147:3

He heals the brokenhearted and binds up their wounds.

Introduction

Uncovered. In plain text this term just means "not covered." For a further description Merriam-Webster dictionary explains it as.

: to make known: bring to light: disclose, reveal: uncover the truth.

So, as you may expect that is what I will be doing throughout this book series. When I asked God what was on his heart he simply said, "I am tired of things being hidden." As I tried to understand how I would play a part in the revealing he showed me that parts of my own life had been hidden in the shadows. Therefore, here I am in all my mess. It was the year of 2017 when I first heard from God regarding the start of this series. Since then, life has thrown anything and everything it could my way; I've dodged some bullets while running straight into others and I have the scars to prove it. But all in all, one thing remained: the love of Christ. His love scared me many times because I couldn't hide. The thing is, I'd become so accustomed to burying my wounds that I felt like death was upon me when I was forced to uncover them. Yes, it felt like dying because following Christ means dying to yourself. Your flesh: and it's one of the hardest things I'd ever had to do.

Galatians 5:24

Those who belong to Christ Jesus have crucified the flesh with its passions and desires.

* * *

Whenever I heard people mentioning "dying to self" I applauded their words, but I had no idea what I was truly clapping for. One night, after self-sabotaging yet another event (one where I knew I should've been in attendance) my heart threatened to break out of my chest. It was the most excruciating pain in my life and trust me I've felt heartache many times before. But I'd always felt pain over something external (a family member passing away, a bad fall-out with someone, and so on); yet the agony in my chest was from internal wounds. It was because I had to face myself (deal with me). For years I'd turned the mirror on everyone else while neglecting my own healing process. The Bible says to remove the speck from your own eye before trying to remove someone else's. That scripture had gone over my head on many occasions because I still found myself trying to fix everyone else's life while mine was in shambles. Honestly, I was suffering from guilt and shame. Each time I took a step forward, something from my past would creep up and I'd be bound once again by the chains of fear. Missing that last event was the final straw; the thing that sent me over the edge but in a good way. My mind was made up; I'd allowed the enemy too much say so in my life and I wound no longer be tormented. Therefore, here I am.

My name is DeLisa Treshelle. For years I struggled with a **pornography addiction** which led to feelings of self-doubt, shame, and unworthiness. Those childhood memories were trapped along with the ones I pressed down where I fumbled in the sheets with some of my cousins. **Incest**: we were very young, not even ten years of age when our confused feelings had us exploring prematurely. **STD's.** I got my first one around the age of eighteen, shortly after losing my virginity. Some were incurable while one unfortunately was not, herpes. It snuck up on me and depression came along with it; the kind that made me want to take my own life, again. While in my home, isolated, I sat with the darkness for days in confusion. Understanding was foreign to me because I'd taken several tests for herpes that were negative. So, when I saw that one read positive, there was a deep case of rebuttal. From trying to figure out how it was possible to just wallowing in my despair, I asked God to take me away. Giving away my virtue by losing my virginity at eighteen years old was the thing that sent me over the edge. It became my biggest regret and haunted me for years. So, that is some of my story. Though, it has taken me a while to get here I believe that I am arriving right on time. If you are here, then you are in the very place God wants you to be. You may find something relatable to your own life by reading my narrative. Or yours could be completely different. Whatever the case you are worthy to receive love. That is what I came here to tell you. Because all the things I experienced made me believe I was not good enough for love. Those tormenting memories of childhood sexual encounters, being with other women, giving myself away to different men, and so forth caused me to shrink back, to reduce myself. It is the deep-rooted wounds that keep us away from destiny since we don't like to truly face difficult things. No one wants to really deal with the fact that they had an abortion and it scarred them. That the thoughts of what could have been keep them up at night. Or that the time they were raped or molested caused them to become paralyzed. These are the truths that keep us stagnant. But by uncovering hidden acts we can overcome anything. What is your moment? What is the one thing that shifted the entire direction of your life? Go back to that situation and reflect on it. Do not run away from the pain associated with truly embracing your tragedy. As a matter of fact, grab your journal and write it down or notate it somewhere in your phone; then come back. I'll give you a few seconds...

That may have been difficult. Trust me I know first-hand what it means to ignore the hard things. For me, stopping didn't make any sense so I just kept on moving. Nevertheless, I was going nowhere fast because the things I tried to outrun eventually caught up with me. But I had to learn that nothing happens overnight. Healing takes time and it is not easy at all. Yet, it is the most rewarding. My prayer for you is that God opens the doors of heaven and sends you the support you need during this time. Until then, may you find comfort from reading my story. Welcome to Childhood Scars.

* * *

Writing was always my place of solace. There was no order to what I wrote, but as my pen leaked onto the paper it revealed what I needed to say. Writing made me feel whole and when I journaled the world made more sense.

But I have found that some things I never wrote about. Year after year, I ruffled through the pages of different journals, yet it was as if parts of my life still didn't make any sense. There were so many missing puzzle pieces and I believe that is why I started my search for love. Writing made me want to understand words more so with that I became attracted to reading books. I read all types of stories but of course, romance was my favorite. I was head over heels for the stories. The way the male characters fought for the woman they loved always pulled at my heartstrings. Yet, as I scanned the pages, I found that the stories did not portray what I saw in my own surroundings. There was always a happy ending but when I looked at my own life there wasn't a comparison. For me, the endings were devastating. I read book after book, hoping to find a story like my own. Something that spoke to me. Not quite finding what I was looking for, I latched on to movies. Movies for me were somewhat better because I got to see emotions played out on the big screen. Seeing the characters live and in action fascinated me. But it still wasn't enough. I wanted to understand love. Most of all, I wanted to figure out why I couldn't have the same happy ending as the women I read about. I both loved and hated romance at the same time. There was an adoration simply because I loved to see love, but I couldn't help wondering when my time would come. So, a part of me envied the women I saw in the movies or the ones I read about in my treasured romance novels. Obsessed is the best word to describe it; I was preoccupied with wanting to be loved. So much so that after changing my college degree several times, I finally decided on English Literature because I could study some of the greatest romance stories in History. But I had no idea what love was. Mainly because my view was based on fantasies. I had this dream of having the perfect partner and being the perfect mate but that didn't happen. My story went more like; partnering up with destructive men, being abused but also being abusive, catching sexually transmitted diseases, sleeping with women, and suffering from what seemed to be a never-ending cycle of brokenness. The thing God was trying to show me was that he needed me to deal with me first. I would never be the woman I was supposed to be for anyone until I dealt with my wounds. The things that happened in my childhood affected me. It meant something and no matter how many times I suppressed memories or ran away from my past, something had to change. I had to be willing to evolve and become.

* * *

I once believed that just saying the words I love you meant more than the actions that followed. But love is an action and many times what we hear is not followed by the characteristics of God's love.

1 Corinthians 13:4-8

Love is patient, love is kind. It does not envy, it does not boast, it is not proud. It does not dishonour others, it is not self-seeking, it is not easily angered, it keeps no record of wrongs. Love does not delight in evil but rejoices with the truth. It always protects, always trusts, always hopes, always perseveres.

Love never fails. But where there are prophecies, they will cease; where there are tongues, they will be stilled; where there is knowledge, it will pass away.

* * *

Insecurities always made me feel like I was not enough; pretty enough, smart enough, worthy enough. Those thoughts threatened to rip my very existence into shreds. They were lies that the enemy had whispered to me since childhood. But while those inadequacies tried to steal my wholeness, God urged me to walk in freedom. Christ had the final say so in my life and it is the same for you. My story was already written and predestined, before my mother gave birth to me, I just had to believe that.

* * *

Restoration of Israel

Jeremiah 30: 1-2

This is the word that came to Jeremiah from the Lord: "This is what the Lord, the God of Israel, says: 'Write in a book all the words I have spoken to you.

An Entry from My Journal: February 11. 2020

Write it down even if it hurts. Showing emotions is not a sign of weakness because being vulnerable leads to wholeness. Someone made a Facebook live video yesterday, and the assignment was to write down all your insecurities, say them out loud, and speak against them. I will be honest, I have yet to do it. Why? Because stating insecurities does not feel good. Everyone wants to appear strong, but we shorten our growth by skipping steps. Without a secure foundation, everything around you will be at risk. So, write it down even if it hurts. Allow God the opportunity to heal the internal parts of you; the deep places that you don't want to admit are unsteady.

Your words are your weapon and there is power in sharing your story.

Writing Heals.

Preface

An Entry from My Journal: April 9, 2016

Today is a new day and it has been eye-opening, to say the least. So many journeys have come and gone. Lessons learned, challenges. I often wonder when my time will come. When will I find true peace and happiness? I have been lost for so long that I don't even know how much time has passed; could be months, could be years. I do know that my life looks nothing like I'd planned it out to be. I miss my grandmother and I need her guidance. I need her calm spirit to breathe hope into me again. I know that I need God, but I have no idea how to go about seeking him. My chest is weighed down with depression and anxiety. I once believed that love was all I needed but love does not seem attainable for me. When I look in the mirror, I see such a dismantled person that sometimes I think it would be better if I were to disappear from the earth, completely. I just can't catch a break. This health condition has truly ruined my life. I'm tired of looking at my legs in disgust. I see no beauty in them when they were once my greatest assets.

Everything is falling apart, and I can't do anything but lie here while the bricks fall one by one. Where is my knight and shining armor? When will my stability come? In all areas, not just one; mentally, emotionally, physically, spiritually, and financially. I long to have a happy life while maintaining a pure soul. I just wish I knew where to start but maybe this is it, jotting down my hopes, dreams, fears, and insecurities in yet another journal.

No one really taught me how to have a relationship with God, so it is difficult to connect with him. There was more emphasis on being a good woman or finding a good man than walking with Christ. But through all of this, I want to start a new chapter in my life. Today is the day that I stop procrastinating. I will stay up all night writing, learning how to love myself, and practicing positivity. I will learn to forgive and be kind towards others. Compassionate and caring. These are my most fearful thoughts. The ones I'm afraid to speak out loud for the fear of failure. Yet, I want to write them down anyway. One day I will be a great wife and mother, a successful writer, and the owner of a book publishing company. It is April 4, 2016, I am twenty-six years old, and today is the start of my life. God, I pray that you will take away my regrets and replace them with your peace, joy, understanding, and love. I promise to let go of the four-year relationship that I know is not for me. I will find beauty in the simple things and my new hearts' desire is to one day share my story with the world. As the tears dry up from my face tonight, I will pray for restoration. I'm tired of holding on to the past and dealing with these constant battles within my mind. I'm tired of living in fear; fear of failure, fear of death, fear of revealing my condition, fear of rejection, fear of loss, fear of everything. This constant state of anxiety will not break me. Not anymore. God, I give it all to you.

PART ONE

Childhood Recollections

1

A Young Girl Trapped

God is love. How often do we forget that truth or refuse to acknowledge it at all? Had I really understood the true meaning of love, it may have saved me some heartache. Then again heartache is what brought me to the feet of Jesus.

I had spent years trying to heal myself as a grown woman; only to realize that the little girl who felt abandoned by her father and rejected by her mother was the one who really needed to be healed.

* * *

Shreveport. La 1996

I thought granny's house could withstand anything; it was a single-family home that stood north of a rock filled driveway held together by a weary porch. With the neighborhood being so intimate, our neighbors were more like family. So, it did not matter who walked down the street, everyone spoke to them with a familiar tone in their voice.

Our little part of the city was not a wealthy area. In fact, there was more poverty surrounding us than anything else. Yet, money was the least of our issues because deeper circumstances such as rape, molestation, incest, physical abuse and more spread from home to home. But those hidden things could not stay in the dark for long; at least until now. The grownups didn't seem to mind the turmoil; they wore their scars proudly. We had to 'stay in a child's place' but that doesn't mean we didn't tune our ears to the door to overhear many things such as one woman sleeping with another woman's husband, family members bedding one another, domestic violence and so on. Everything they talked about seemed to be okay; accepted even. We heard many stories growing up but of course, as children, we hardly understood them. While some made us laugh hysterically, most of them were heart wrenching. Looking back, I could see how so many things had come to destroy our families.

* * *

Granny sat at the front window on most days. Her dark brown eyes were laced with a blue ring around them, and they'd seen some troubled times; but she still tried her best to help those in need. She seemed to be searching for lost souls. The ones who everyone else had forgotten about. Or maybe she just sat in worry, either about her own life or the lives of her family members. Her eyes were a compliment to her high cheekbones, cocoa skin, and aging hair. They were the kind of eyes that saw you, beyond your outer appearance or your headstrong personality. Granny was born during the year of the Great Depression; in 1929. She'd dropped out of school in the fourth grade, but life and God became her teachers. She was kind but also fierce.

Shreveport is the melting pot of culture for the surrounding regions, Texas, Louisiana, and Arkansas. But, in my part of town, we had little to no diversity. We saw a lot of people who looked just like us; the same story, the same struggle; and our lives consisted of getting by until the next day. Our bellies were filled with rice, beans, white loaves of bread, greens, neck bones, sometimes noodles, pop tarts, off brand cereal, and Vienna sausages. But, on the good days, granny made her infamous biscuits or bread pudding. She was like the mother of the neighborhood, and everyone came to her house when she cooked.

* * *

A recollection

The aged chair creaked under my small buttocks while my grandmother pressed my wavy textured hair with a hot comb. The wooden floors in her tiny kitchen stayed in place only by the grace of God. Gravity halted you in her home. As steam rose from the hot comb, a stench of the blue hair grease melting lingered in the space. While the other part of the air was pleasantly filled with the scent of granny's homemade biscuits and sugar syrup. Those biscuits fell apart by the slightest touch. I also got a whiff of butter resting in a cast iron skillet. The skillet, like her, were growing older but they both remained strong. She had my mother at forty-years-old so as she straightened my hair her hands refused to remain still. Yet, she never burned me. Granny just casually placed the hot comb on the fire and waved it in the air to cool it before placing the iron on my scalp. My time with her was one of the many things that helped me escape because real life seemed to haunt me.

I saw myself inside of my head. As if a miniature version of me ran around in circles. Restless. I may have created an image of myself there; one that reflected how I felt. There was a burden on my back from feeling like my voice would not matter. I never felt seen. So, I kicked and screamed inside of my mind because I could not do that in real life. I saw myself through her eyes; my own. I believed that if I spoke up again in real life, disappointment would follow my words, so I remained quiet. I wanted to be in my own room even though I had grown to love being at granny's house. It was not my true desire. I accepted it because the times I did speak up about wanting to stay home I never could.

I also had to make sure my younger brother was safe. I did not have to babysit him or anything, but I did try to nurture him. Though, I fell short many times. Because of my own internal battles, I lashed out at him and was very mean more times than I liked to admit. I just knew he was not old enough to understand everything. Since I was older, I took in most of what I saw and to me it seemed like the adults did what made them happy, and we got the scraps. Yes, there was some love, and we had the necessities provided such as food, a roof over our heads, and so on. But I do not recall anyone sitting down to care for us emotionally. If we acted out then a whooping followed, though I did not get many; I witnessed a multitude of them. I believe that children act out for a reason; a missing in action parent, sexual confusion, being torn down verbally and more. *Why doesn't anyone want me?* Followed by *Why doesn't anyone love me?* Were the questions that I asked myself.

I wanted my brother and I to have a real home. One that was filled with love and joy often. I am sure our mother wanted the same, but she couldn't do everything on her own. So, I sat with my back pressed against the hard chair, pushing down my heart's desires. The words I wanted to say flowed away like the waves of an ocean, lost in the ripples. I chose to replace my pain with the love standing behind my back. She made it all better. Our hearts beat as one.

As I glanced at the moon peeking from outside the kitchen curtain the darkness seemed to laugh at me. It had a voice. It told me that I was not enough; and the stars sparkled in agreement.

* * *

My grandma finished with my hair and skirted through the house closing the blinds first. She had made a cotton clothes pin bag out of a checkered pattern, and it hung around her neck. Granny had this weird aura about her; she carried herself with both confidence and defeat.

She cleaned and lit an oil lamp in preparation for bedtime. I stayed in place by the kitchen, awaiting her return. I refused to ask the question I really wanted to. So, I swallowed it down along with the bile that sat in my throat.

Moments later the small tin tub was filled with soap and water. Granny knew I was upset but she never said much about our situation. She just did her best to make us feel cared for. I walked into the bathroom and embraced the coolness of the small tub. It did not matter what time of the year it was, fire still crackled in the background from the many gas heaters placed around granny's home. The smell of burning matches entered my nostrils. We never had long in the bathroom. Granny would be knocking at the door before we even had the chance to take a proper bath. But I always needed my quiet moments. They kept me sane. The girl inside my head laughed and ran until the knocks came. A bit later, grease melted in granny's hands as she placed them in front of the fire. My large saucer eyes lit up in the blue flames, the sparks taking me to another place. Just as many times before, I zoned out as granny greased me down from head to toe. I watched the chipped brown paint on the walls, fantasizing about another place. I thought of the upcoming day and how we would be awakened early in the morning for breakfast. My little brother cried in the background, breaking my concentration; "I want my mama, I want my mama," over and over like one of those records' mama had but to no avail. I already knew she was not coming to get us. We had been fooled just like many other times before.

I tossed and turned in my thick cotton pajamas before getting up to use the restroom. I had no idea what the time was, but I saw the sun peeking in the window. Its glow shined over the edge of Granny's night gown. Her room was separate from ours and she closed the door off, so I had to look inside. There she was, up with the chickens sitting in her favorite chair. While her bible lay across her lap, a cup of water sat beside her feet along with her spit cup. I groggily went to get some water out of the kitchen and made my way back to our side of the house.

* * *

Those feelings of rejection from my mother followed me to school. I was very timid and did not like to talk too much. Elementary was frightening for me but I had some hope that I would make a friend one day. As children scattered everywhere, most of them ventured off into groups to find their perspective places; already being connected from the previous year. I faded into the background because I did not fit in. Noticing that the other girls had light skin and pretty hair, I did not believe they would like me because I was teased before. So, my identity came from who my peers said I was. If they said I was ugly then it had to be true. If they did not accept me, how could I accept myself? Self-love was non-existent for me. I wanted to get attention from the popular boys because they were cute and had all the latest fashions. But I had no idea what they went through at home. Popularity was based on ignorance and naivety. After all, every kid in school was battling with something. Regardless of our outer appearance there were things going on in our childhood homes. Secrets that in a way linked us together. While I was struggling with feeling unloved mingled with my confused sexual hormones, other kids were suffering in silence from things as well, while their parents really had money issues because they were trying so hard to keep up with the joneses. However, in all our problems we never had any real discussions about them. Things would fly out in arguments but there was no plan for a resolve. We did not go to therapy. We went to church. But once the doors of the Church house closed, our problems were still there, lacing the paint inside our homes with despair, regret, broken dreams, and insecurities.

While I was growing up, I never heard anyone talking about purpose and that we were all created by God for a specific reason. For years, I had no idea who I was, and I believe that is part of the reason why I wanted to commit suicide so many times. I felt that removing myself from hard situations would be much better than suffering through them. But each time, Christ showered me with his presence or sent an angel to stop me.

Jeremiah 29:11

For I know the plans I have for you, declares the Lord, plans to prosper you and not to harm you, plans to give you hope and a future.

2

A Girl Meshed with Family

An Entry from My Journal: February 12, 2020

WHEN I WAS YOUNGER, I believed what others said about me because I thought they knew best. I made their insults my truth. But everything makes sense now. God, you did not take me through those things to harm me and regardless of how it felt, your presence was always there. I remember the pull I felt when I went to Church but I was unclear on what it was because religion had me bound. You have been building my testimony for some time and the gifts you placed inside of me started at a young age. I dribbled in my notebooks and drew figures and now I'm a Prophetic Artist. Words would pour out of me from my experiences and now I am an author. You make no mistakes, and it was all in preparation for my destiny. I ran from this for so long, but I know that I must be vulnerable and reveal my true story. I have faith in you God. I pray you light the path for me so that I may walk in true freedom. In Jesus name. Amen.

Jeremiah 29: 12-14

Then you will call on me and come and pray to me, and I will listen to you. You will seek me and find me when you seek me with all your heart. I will be found by you," declares the Lord, "and will bring you back from captivity. I will gather you from all the nations and places where I have banished you," declares the Lord, "and will bring you back to the place from which I carried you into exile."

* * *

There is an evil pull going on in the world and up until recently I walked around in a trance as if I had no purpose. Whenever I branched out to do what God called me to do, I stopped. My soul cried out, but I refused to seek solace in Christ completely because the word of God seemed to be dismantled. So, I was fearful of seeking the word for myself. Prayer and fasting was a part of many seasons but anytime I felt a tug to dig deeper, I reneged. I did not know that God had all the power to turn my situation around because that would have required more faith and trust. However, once I meditated on his words through the bible, they spoke to me, and what I felt was irrefutable because I could not deny the power within them. The holy spirit is real and once I had an encounter with the holy ghost my life changed forever. It did not matter what society was telling me to do, I had to address the call on my life. My purpose had been trapped by childhood trauma, old church wounds, venomous relationships, a lack of confidence in who I belonged to, and overall

Fear. My release started to happen when I did the very thing that made me the most uncomfortable, Writing this book. I know that does not even make any sense, right? I am an author and Manuscript Delivery Coach, so I write all the time. But it was not just any publication that I had an issue with. My struggle was with this book series. It felt like God wanted me to remove the human parts of myself and open my life up for scrutiny. It was one thing to write down how I felt and go over my life in my head. But, sharing that with other people felt insane. Though, even in my doubts, I reflected on the scripture that promised good plans for my future. **Jeremiah 29:11.**

* * *

Regardless of what happened in my childhood, I continued to move forward, oblivious to how it was affecting me inside. I believed that if I didn't acknowledge things then maybe I could just forget they ever took place. But trauma has a way of sticking with you, even while you're living in a state of denial. The things you promised to take to your grave, the internal vows you made to yourself will show up in your life some way. Even if you never say them out loud, they will still affect you. Inwardly those experiences within my family made me feel undeserving of love. So, instead of me waiting until I could be found by a true man of God, I settled for broken men because they were just like me. We were mirror images of one another trying to fix our wounds by having sex.

Harboring hidden things determines how you live your life, how you treat others, and how you treat yourself. But I want to talk to the offender and the victim for a minute. If you were the one who caused harm to someone else just know that God still loves you and it is time for you to forgive yourself. We don't hear this often, but Christ loves the offender just as he loves the victim. Maybe you experienced the same thing where someone touched you inappropriately and it made you believe that was okay to do. I fear that you may be reading this, and no one has ever told you that you must heal from those wounds. Maybe people taught you to just live your life as if nothing ever happened. Or because you were harmed by someone very close to you, a part of you felt as if you did something to deserve the treatment. Your mother, your father, your brother, your cousin, your uncle, your aunt, a close family friend; any of these people could have been your first offender. So, you went on while you were still uncertain, while you were still unhealed and hurt. It is also possible that you knew what you were doing, and you intentionally inflicted pain on others because you were suffering. Even in that, you must release yourself because God still has a purpose for you as well. Was it a horrible thing to do? Yes, but no longer can you live in condemnation, fear, and discomfort. I bind up the hand of the enemy in your life and I declare that you are free. I pray that God starts to heal your mind from all the tormenting memories you replay over and over in your head. The ones that no one else knows about. Those occurrences that internally make you want to take your own life because the wounds are too deep. I need you to know that there is more for you. Regardless of where you are in your life. You may be in jail, in the streets, a pillar in your community, the CEO of a successful company, or a regular worker; wherever you are Christ has found you. Come out of the shadows; ask God to reveal the reasons why you did what you did and once you do, relieve yourself from all the guilt you have been carrying. Free yourself by going back to make amends. If you don't do anything else, go apologize to the people you have hurt. Do not go on as if it didn't happen. The people you harmed may appear to be living good lives, but you aren't. You're suffocating and trying to use anything you can to cope. But it won't go away, will it? That is because it was never meant to be brushed under the rug. The things you have done have to be brought to a light. Hear me. Do not miss your opportunity to take the right course of action. This is your encouragement, but it is also a warning. Do it now.

James 5:16

Therefore, confess your sins to each other and pray for each other so that you may be healed. The prayer of a righteous person is powerful and effective.

*** *** ***

To the victim. I know that you have lived your life in secret because you were afraid of what the truth would reveal. You may feel like it's too late to come out. Maybe no one will believe you or maybe they won't even care. Trust me I have heard it all. When I started to share my story publicly the opinions of others caused me to retreat once again.

"Why wait all of these years to speak up?"

"You must be lying"

"You should heal for yourself and keep your business private."

The list goes on and one but guess what? The enemy will use anyone he can get his hands on to shut you up. This isn't the season to be silent for you have been quiet long enough. So, I declare that even as you are reading this your mind is becoming freer. I pray that God speaks to you in a new way through this book and that it will be no doubt that the words written are directly from him. Let me first tell you that what happened to you is not your fault. It wasn't anything you wore or the way you swung your hips. You didn't encourage it to happen. What if I told you that you just got caught in the crossfires of someone else's brokenness or their inability to not recognize the enemy at work within them? Rage, lust, and perversion are just a few spirits the enemy uses to control people; and whether they are willing vessels, or innocent bystanders it all hurts the same, doesn't it? This may be hard for you to hear but you must forgive your offender. Better yet, it is time for you to forgive yourself because of the actions you made based on what happened to you.

Freedom is your portion, but you cannot obtain

it until you let go. This doesn't mean that what

they did was okay. It just means you deserve to

live a life of peace. One that isn't weighed down

by regrets and past mistakes. You may not ever

get the apology that you deserve. But this one is

for you.

Psalm 86:5

You, Lord, are forgiving and good, abounding in love to all who call to you.

* * *

Shreveport, La 1998

We were a close-knit family; woven together like a quilt. It was as if Granny's prayers glued us all together. We sang to the beat of our own drum. When one person laughed, everyone laughed; and the few times we cried, we sat together to comfort one another. As if we were all sharing the same heartbreak.

Matthew 6: 9-14

This, then, is how you should pray:

Our Father in heaven, hallowed be your name, your kingdom come, your will be done, on earth as it is in heaven. Give us today our daily bread. And forgive us our debts, as we also have forgiven our debtors. And lead us not into temptation but deliver us from the evil one. For if you forgive other people when they sin against you, your heavenly Father will also forgive you.

* * *

That prayer hung on granny's wall along with the ten commandments next to the front door. We had to say it out loud each night before bedtime. My cotton pajamas were still my favorite and I cuddled up next to my cousins in the rollaway bed or the second bedroom.

The second bedroom. What happened there was a part of my childhood that I wanted to forget; but I couldn't. Growing up the term "hunching" was thrown around like it was just a normal thing for a child to do. I never had an adult to sit me down and talk to me about it. Though, if someone got caught hunching, they would get a whooping. However, that was the only consequence. I found that when a kid got in trouble for hunching, they'd go right back and do it again. Because the adults wouldn't take the time to deal with what was going on. Anytime an occurrence took place, it wasn't talked about for very long. My cousins and I didn't really know what we were doing. Of course, anything we tried was based off the things we'd seen. There were several pornography tapes at different homes and of course those were the things that pulled us in. My addiction started at a very young age. Before the age of ten I was already addicted to pornography, and I didn't know how to stop it or really deal with it. The scenes were vivid. What I saw was nothing like the PG scenes that came across the television in an adult movie. In the regular movies there may have been a hint of what happened, but it was never full blown. However, what we saw was full blown and it was well beyond our years. We explored prematurely and a bit innocently trying to fan the flames of our raging hormones. We'd sneak around behind the adults back and still moments with each other in the middle of the night. Though, we went to Church like every week, living double lives. We had our secrets even as children so there is no telling what the adults were hiding. Even in church, no one was talking about the destruction of pornography or any of the inappropriate things that were happening in our families. No, things like that were not even acknowledged and since no one was saying anything, I just believed God was okay with it.

We went on as normal, laughing through the prayers each night before bed.

Luke 12: 3

What you have said in the dark will be heard in the daylight, and what you have whispered in the ear in the inner rooms will be proclaimed from the roofs.

* * *

At times, I wanted to understand the word of God. Especially because granny read the bible to us so much. Other times I became angry because it was another thing pushed on to me where I had no say so.

Church was never an option. I believe that is why we took advantage of our free time. In between our secret moments in the bed, we played often, whether it was taking trips to the Lil' store, playing under the house, walking, and picking blackberries, making mock-up food out of grass, or riding our bikes. We made our time together fun and memorable.

Although, the adults did not have to go to Church, most of them still went out of obedience to granny and because it made her happy. However, my mama was a different breed, and she had a mind of her own. Being the youngest of her siblings, she mostly did what she wanted and got away with it. Grandma watched her skirt out of the door, on several Sundays, making it known that she was going home to sleep. Her Saturday nights out had probably taken a toll.

Our clothes were in short supply, but granny was resourceful. So, instead of us getting new dresses, she hand-washed the ones we already had; and the boys repeated their slacks and dress shirts. Granny washed our limited wardrobe on a worn washboard; then she hung them out to dry on the clothing line she had put up in the backyard. After she rung out the water with her hands, the sun soaked up any remaining water.

One of my main dresses was baby pink; the thickness of the fabric was already enough to hide my private areas, but granny was old school. So, regardless of the material, a slip had to be worn underneath the dress as well. My dress was matched with either white stockings or white ruffle socks; sometimes both; completed with white leather shoes.

* * *

Broken lyrics flowed out of the mouths of our entire church congregation; less than one hundred people. We opened our mouths and sang about how the blood of Jesus saved us because he died on the cross. Sundays were repetitive. The sermons were recycled, the songs were stale, and the people looked trapped, especially the adults.

Most of the time, I stared at the colorful stained windows where I again fantasized about being somewhere else. I did find some humor in one thing though. In fact, all of us laughed as a short heavy-set lady sang about 'wings' which she pronounced 'wangs' and how if she had wangs she would not be there because she would be in heaven. I believe we found it so amusing because she was missing a few of her front teeth. But it was no laughing matter. That church was miserable from the pastor on down. Yet, we made do. I sang in the choir along with my brother and a few of my cousins. One of our songs of choice was silver and gold by Kirk Franklin. Our little mouths flung out the words as if we wrote the lyrics.

But I still did not know God. I just knew what granny said about him. Yet, he had to be something majestic because her entire life surround around his son, Jesus Christ. She said that everything was because of him, and her bible rarely left her arms. Her favorite one was given to her in 1993 by her daughter who had been incarcerated for many years. She was the eldest living child and most of granny's prayers were sent up to God for her release.

* * *

My pink dress may have been pretty, but I didn't think I was. Mostly because I was hardly ever told that by anyone. I felt ugly and awkward. Even as I laughed, sang, and played with my family. I always thought my mama was though and everyone else agreed. They loved the way she dressed and her natural-full-body-shape. Even the young boys at school teased me about she couldn't have been my mother. Her short hair only accentuated her brown eyes, small face, and straight teeth. I always thought my mama favored Nia Long but her gold teeth made her unique. There was a letter engraved in it that represented her first name. People complimenting my mama just made me feel even more insecure; and those feelings grew. It was on my heart on many occasions, to open-up to her but she wasn't around during the times I wanted to talk. So, when she was there, I had already become resentful.

The walls I placed around myself grew higher and higher. While, in the center of my family, I hardly spoke of my true feelings. It felt better that way. If I did not reveal anything then I did not have to expect anything in return, such as love or comfort. My loneliness suffocated me and everyone else seemed to have somebody to lean on. My mama had her guy friends. My brother had his daddy. My cousins and peers had their clicks of friends; and granny had her bible. All I had was myself and my thoughts.

***

Holidays and birthdays were the hardest because I longed to have my daddy around.

Though mama always made sure we had grand birthday celebrations; it did not erase the need for my other parent. At Christmas time though, the ache was a little more bearable because my uncle stepped in. I will never forget the cabbage patch doll I received one year. Her porcelain skin and fluffy golden hair was done up with light curls. My other grandmother also stepped in to compensate for my father not being there. She would come and pick me up during the summers in her red sports car. We traveled from the Cooper Road to Karnack Texas over several dirt roads. Sometimes, we went to Dallas to see my aunt and my other cousins. My brother tagged along if he was not staying with his dad for the summer. He loved hanging with my grandma.

She would blast blues songs for most of the ride with a beer in her lap.

My grandma tried her best to talk to me about my daddy, but I really did not want to hear it. I listened to be polite, but it went in one ear and out the other. I could tell she was upset by my nonchalance, though, it didn't matter to me. I would not hear any excuses about my father's absence. I wondered where he was when I was getting touched by my older female cousin as we spent the nights in Dallas.

She was about fourteen while I was around the age of nine. I didn't think that any of it was wrong so I can't say that she coerced me into anything. Since it had already happened back home, I just believed that was the way things were supposed to be. So, no, I didn't want to hear anything about my father; because he was nowhere to be found amid everything I'd experienced. I was angry and felt entitled to my feelings because the two people I needed love from; had chosen other things to occupy their time.

3

An Older Girl Trapped

YOUR PARENTS NEED FORGIVENESS TOO. For me, it was easier to let things go when it came to a relationship. I would allow hurt to pile up from emotional and physical abuse only to push it back down. But even after I fought and cursed, I still found myself back in the bed or still entertaining the relationship. Covering up wounds with lies, kisses, and sexual impurities. Both me and whatever partner I had at the time harboring unhealed wounds. As I lie there, I could feel the heaviness leaking from them; invisible blood spilling out over the bed. Over time, it made me think of the ones who created me. What wounds did they have that were just covered up with a band-aid although major surgery was required? Not to mention they created children when they were still growing up themselves.

How it must have been for my mama raising two children in her twenties. She had lost her father shortly before finding out she was pregnant with me. Maybe she was searching for love too and stayed during the abuse longer because the need to have her children taken care of took precedence. But, for the longest time, I did not see it that way. I never thought about what my father's childhood could have been like either. What was he facing as a young man trying to find his way in the world? No, I only saw my own pain and frustrations which was fine while I was still a child. But as an adult I had to learn that I was the one responsible for my own life. My own healing.

1 Corinthians 13:11

When I was a child, I talked like a child, I thought like a child, I reasoned like a child. When I became a man, I put the ways of childhood behind me.

***

Shreveport. La 1999

My Mother's hands were not as gentle as granny's. I scooted and wiggled in the chair whenever the heat from her hot comb came near my face. Her determined yet sad eyes bore into me as I was chastised for moving too much. I did not stop to take notice back then, but the signs were always there. The emptiness. The fight. The hope. The pain. The loss. The love. As the hot comb nudged my ear, my hair seized from the temperature and the grease. I would always have little burnt marks at the top of my ears whenever my mama pressed my hair.

We never really spoke about what was going on much in our home. Though, the adults in my family huddled at times to fight the man my mama was with. But I never saw her draft up a plan for escape. It just seemed like his behavior was accepted and 'okay'. Sure, she cried out and screamed that she was tired, but we still stayed. Our burglar bar door could not protect us from what was going on inside our home. The threat there was almost worse than anything coming in from the outside. I lived in fear every day that something worse than what was happening would occur. I panicked in my sleep because I didn't know if my mama would live to see the next day. How many times would he abuse her before going too far? Because we didn't know what to expect, I really didn't even know what to think.

***

I pretended I lived outside of that small rectangular home. Maybe I could escape to the backyard. There was a fence there which separated our house from the apartments south of us. It's where my aunt and cousins lived. I knew I could have more freedom there as well. My mother never understood why I was so distant and closed off, but I did. You would think a parent would try to figure out why their child is a certain way but that rarely happened growing up. If we didn't listen, caught an attitude, stomped our feet, or any of those things; a whooping or punishment followed. Yet, there were so many traumatic events happening around us and no one was offering a solution. They didn't even think there was a problem, with anything. Most of the things we experienced happened to them and they believed they "turned out just fine." So, how could they have true compassion for us? When they thought we had it easier than they did?

***

There was a song my mama sang every time it came on the radio. 'When a Woman's Fed Up' by R. Kelly. It sprang through her speakers over and over but once the sun rose on the next day we were still in the same house. There was no packing of bags or arrangements to relocate. No plans to kick him out. No plans to protect our hearts from being broken at the sight of seeing our mother broken. Or at least what I knew of. My thoughts of us making a run for mama's 1985 cream Grand Prix with the peanut butter top never happened and my dreams were crushed.

My brother expressed his emotions more outwardly than me and we laid in bed together when things got too bad. Well, most of the time he was in my room anyway. I did not know it at the time, but he could have found comfort in being next to me because I served as his protection. I can only imagine what was going through his mind. One time, he threatened to go and fight our stepdad for abusing our mama. It was funny then because he was so young and little. But our situation was no laughing matter.

The times that we were not in my room or his we would watch TV in the living room because it was further away from the chaos. The floor TV there was also the biggest one in the house. But the walls were thin, and our little ears pricked up every time a fight or argument broke out, whether we had company or not. The movies we watched may have taken us to another place, but it was only temporary.

Our stepdad did not seem to care about children being in the home. I don't even think he was conscious enough to realize anything though because once he got drunk all hell broke loose and mama became the outlet for his insecurities. Ironically though, he was kind when he was not holding a bottle in his hands. We were spoiled with a home and material things, but it did not remove the internal wounds. He loved old school R & B, especially the mushy songs. K-Ci and JoJo will forever be implanted in my brain because of how much he played their songs. His oversized brown van had various tapes lying around. Ones by artists that I grew up to love. It was crazy how our stepdad played so many love songs, yet he could not properly love my mama. But I now know that he must have been dealing with his own share of trauma. After all, it takes a hurt person to hurt someone else. Somewhere along the line he may have lost himself and was unable to give her the type of love she deserved. My brother and I were grateful for the peaceful times with our mama. The times we got to sit and watch TV with her. When she was allowed to be just a twenty something year old woman with two children. We had so many movie tapes. They lined the oversized cabinet and were diversified in different genres. We watched several a day, but I'll always remember this one. *What's Love Got to do with it?* As we tuned in, I took note of my mama's emotions and the change in her breathing. She seemed to relate heavily to that movie which made a lot of sense, because of her situation. The biopic about Tina Turner showed that she used music to pour her pain into. I don't know what my mama used to cope with her distress. But I figured she just dealt with it in her own way. I do, however, recall envying the actress in that movie. Rage flowed over my flesh because of how she broke free. That is all I wanted for us. To be free and secure. I wanted my mama to find a new love so she could be happy; and maybe we could've been happy too.

Inside my head I fought for Mama. My skin stung with anger and desperation to prove there was a better life for me out there. I knew there had to be a better man somewhere in the world for her. I also felt sorry for my mama. I could tell she really didn't want to be in the situation. She was always a different person without him around, more at peace. The other part of me was livid. I didn't understand why we couldn't just leave or why he couldn't leave. I wanted a real Dad. One that was loving and caring not only to us but to her. One that we could watch movies with and laugh. One that told me I was enough. One that told her she was enough. I had given up on my own Daddy. Gave up on the hope that I would ever get what I needed from him. I was past the stage of wanting to be saved by him. Past the stage of needing him.

I made a mental note that I wouldn't be anything like my mama. I would be the opposite of everything she was because I thought she was weak. I believed that I would never go through the types of things she did. But life has a way of making a liar and a believer out of you. *The apple doesn't fall too far from the tree*, they say. My mama was my root and since I never dealt with my childhood, as an adult I went through the same things she did. It went against the very things I swore I would never do.

***

As a kid, I never really heard my mama calling out for Jesus the way our granny did. Then again, I was in my head so much I would not have noticed. There is also the possibility that she was struggling to have a relationship with Christ too. But the way Granny always spoke so highly of his spirit, I thought he could be the key to helping us out of our situation sooner. Yet, what did I know? I was just a child

and children *stayed in a child's place*.

PART TWO

A Virgin No More

4

A Girl Feeling Herself

An Entry from my Journal: Aug 21. 2021

A FEW MONTHS AGO, I wrote in my journal about how worrying had become my idol. God spoke that to me so clearly as I was reading my daily devotional. It is as if anything the holy spirit tells me, I refuse to believe it. Especially if it is something big that requires a level of faith that I am not comfortable with. Then, I go months on end battling in my mind (double mindedness) about what he already revealed to be true. I remember sitting in prayer one day as I was struggling with something. God told me that I do hear voices but not all voices are from him. I also hear voices based on my insecurities, fear, and worrying more and that is what I accept because the bad is more prevalent than the good (my faith). God told me something a few years ago and when it came around again, I forfeited my single season to make it happen faster. I started to idolize what I believed God spoke to me and I put so much focus on what he said instead of continuing with what he wanted me to do in that season. And because of that decision I have unforgiveness towards myself that just will not go away. That period of my life triggered years of self-hate that I'd held against myself unknowingly. I have been getting pulled to heal for months on end, but I keep running away from the process. The scripture I was led to today is:

Ephesians 4:32

Be kind and compassionate to one another, forgiving each other, just as in Christ God forgave you.

God has already forgiven me, but I am having a hard time forgiving myself. Because I thought I had it all together and I did not. I was judgmental, prideful, unkind, a liar, and a manipulator. So, instead of me focusing on myself and my own shortcomings I judged others and called out the things in them I thought they should work on instead of turning the mirror towards myself. This caused me to hurt a lot of people amid battling my own internal wounds. The hardest thing for me to forgive is the fact that I dragged other people along based on my struggle with being called. I know I should let it go and release myself, but I don't know-how. I understand it is a sin to keep myself hostage when Christ has already set me free, but these chains are getting tighter and tighter. I have no compassion or grace towards myself. "Just as Christ God forgave you." That part keeps sticking out to me. It is so hard for me to accept God's love and know that he cared so much for me to forgive me before I ever made any mistakes. I also do not know how to be truthful to the people I have hurt and those lies have held me hostage. I pray that one day I will be able to break free from these bondages.

***

I questioned what love frequently because everything around me was twisted. People would say they loved each other but treated each other with disdain. There was a lack of kindness. My mama was told 'I Love You' but she was being abused at the same time. My father said he loved me in all his letters, yet he was never around. Mothers told their children they loved them in my hood all the while beating them profusely. The boys at school said they loved multiple girls at one time. My view on the subject was just distorted. Even though curiosities pulled at me, I told myself that I would never fall into the same traps of those around me. I wanted something special, and I would wait for it if I had to.

Shreveport, La 2005

Everyone around me was 'doing it.' I sat oddly in the corner listening to the girls at school talk about their first times. Sex wasn't a secret, but I still did not know much about it. Other than what I saw in porno videos. Honestly, I was not that caught up on having the experience for myself in real life, yet I couldn't ignore the desires in my body for much longer. Everything felt different and those feelings made me crave intimacy with a man. I was older, so, I did not have to close my eyes anymore during the sex scenes. Even though as a kid, I still peeked through my fingers to catch glimpses of what was going on in front of the adults. Little did they know, I had seen things way worse than what the PG movies were showing. But as a child, I had no idea what I was really watching. Yet, watching people be intimate caused me to fall into the trap of masturbation. However, in my heart I wanted to be in love before I gave my body to a man. Maybe, I was always a hopeless romantic. Because I felt as if sexual intimacy should be extraordinary, and in a way perfect. Those memories from my childhood tried to resurface but I would always push them down. Though, your body keeps count of everything. So, while I may not have been consciously thinking about certain situations, they still played a part in my choices.

I was afraid to talk about any of my feelings in detail with anyone because of the embarrassment. I thought sex was shameful and that my curiosities should remain hidden. I had also built-up years of shame from watching porn and I believed that addiction should remain hidden.

My mama always told me to let her know when I was ready for sex, but I never wanted to involve her. I also was not prepared and didn't know when I would be. So, I made a silent vow that I would hold out until I felt something special with someone. For me, it had to be exceptional. I refused to experience anything less than the perfect fantasy I'd conjured up for myself.

***

Sex made me apprehensive and even at sixteen I was still very hesitant about acting it out. At that time, I knew a little more about God and his word. One thing that was heavily spoken against in church was sex before marriage. Though, not many people around me were waiting. Over half of us were conceived during premarital sex. Regardless, I wanted my experience to be right and I wanted it to be different.

The act itself just flat out scared me. There was also the fact that anytime a girl gave their virtue away drama seemed to come along with it. But sex or the idea of it was everywhere. On television, in my neighborhood, in my family.

However, when I watched TV, some of the stories were a bit different from what I saw in my neighborhood. At times, the young women on the screen had men that cared about them in return. Whereas I witnessed girls being misused, lied on, lied to, and manipulated. Instead of a boy showing their love for them, they were being broken down physically and mentally. Girls at school were getting into fights over the same boys almost every day. Another broken heart. Another girl trying to find her worth in the opposite sex, and sometimes the same sex. More than likely because her father was missing in action, either by death, incarceration, issues with their mom, or a singular choice.

On the flip side, the boys were probably missing love as well. In our hood there were not many good male role models. Yes, the men worked and took care of home, but some were also cheaters and extremely abusive. We were all living in a whirlwind from our parents' brokenness and their lack of healing.

***

I hated to admit it, but I was starting to have thoughts about my biological father more frequently. At an age where I was longing for companionship, I needed to know how to be a lady. I needed to know what I should expect from men and what I was supposed to give to them. We had a new stepfather but for years, we did not talk much. So, I never sought out his advice. He was a reminder that my real father was not there, and I had too much pride to confide in him.

During it all, I kept feeling pulled to God's word. But I ignored it. My frustrations of misunderstanding the text took over. Then, I just gave up on the idea all together because of what people were doing in church. The ones in church seemed to be worse than the people on the streets. Seeing the things I saw, made me both confused and upset. It pushed me further away from Christ because if I could not trust people, then how could I trust him?

My childhood preacher stood in the pulpit but at home he abused our first lady. His pounding fists left marks on her face that were covered up by lies and a bad makeup job. Most of the men around me were mistreating women and it made me nauseous. I could not understand where the disconnect came from. What would make a man treat a woman with such disgrace?

The questions I had and the longing for my own father didn't do anything but bring me more pain. So, I closed myself off in my room; allowing music, doodling, journaling, and reading to become my therapy. I got lost in the stories I read and the songs I listened to. They were either very much like my own story or fantasies that I wished could come true.

There was one song that I played over and over. Because of you by Kelly Clarkson. I listened to that CD so much and watched the video so many times that I knew each scene before it appeared across the television screen. The lyrics spoke to me because it was exactly how I felt not having my father around. So much so, that I believed it was written just for me. Her words touched my soul. The melodies rang loudly in my ear. "Treshelle, turn that music down." My mother would yell. I obeyed, begrudgingly. She didn't know I had it so loud to drown out the chaos, on the inside.

***

I made a similar vow to myself. I could stay on the sidewalk because I would not get hurt there. I put blocks around my heart so that no pain could seep in. But that action also blocked me from receiving love. Living a life in pretense was better than accepting my reality. I made a promise that I would only trust in myself. I would be the best mother once I got older. I wouldn't abandon them like my father, and I wouldn't reject them like my mother. I would love and cherish them.

I did find it hard to let anyone get too close. But I was conflicted. The wall I'd placed around me left me in a state of uncertainty, because I both resented and longed for love at the same time. I wanted closeness but I also wanted distance. Guys weren't knocking down my door to date me, but I still wished someone would show interest. They rarely talked to me; unless it was in a friendly, homeboy/homegirl kind of way. If I did like a boy, the feeling was hardly ever mutual. It was like I had to bend over backwards to be seen. My childhood scars were starting to appear, and I had no idea what to do because I believed I would never be liked as much as the other girls. It was the same thing I had experienced as a kid; being looked over for someone else. I had no idea what the future held for me, but High School was a place I couldn't wait to leave.

***

As time went on, I was unable to suppress my curiosities. So, I opened myself up to the possibility of love. Someone had to take notice, but I thought they needed help, so I walked around with an invisible sign on my head that read 'pick me, pick me.'

Once some attention started to roll in, I found myself making up feelings. I thought if I said 'I love you' then I could hear those words in return, and it would help fill the void. However, I never felt anything real for the guys I talked to. Even though I believed I did at the time. It was all innocent for me; just a few games, but I found myself in situations that were unexpected

because those boys wanted sex.

5 My First Time

I used to wonder about God's grace. The questions that I had were endless. How could he truly forgive me for having sex before I got married? What about the times I laid with women? The times I covered up the blood of Jesus with multiple sexual encounters. Or the time I found out I had a std my first month into boot camp? How could God look at me with love when I couldn't even look at myself?

***

I'd relished in the feelings of arousal but afterwards I still felt like crap. Though, I was never after long-term satisfaction; just enough pleasure to take my mind off whatever I was dealing with at the time. That thought process was a far cry from my original intentions when it came to sex. I just wanted to be loved and I found myself mixing up the two; just as the women around had done. But as I learned the word of God, I understood that he knew my heart the entire time. So, regardless of my actions, he never questioned the real me.

***

It took some time to start the journey of becoming who I was called to be. I was scared yet excited to meet that version of myself. Over the years, I'd fasted and prayed so many times because I believed that faith would erase all my pain. But I would still walk out of my prayer closet in defeat. I could not for the life of me understand God's love and forgiveness. How could I have lived so recklessly? Those questions left me in a pit of self-hate. I struggled to believe that my sins were wiped clean.

***

Isaiah 1:18

Come now, let us settle the matter, says the Lord. Though your sins are like scarlet, they shall be as white as snow; though they are red as crimson, they shall be like wool.

***

The enemy wanted me to believe that I would was damaged goods, but he was a liar. No amount of sex or sin could ever make God love me any less. For I knew that the enemy only comes to kill, still and destroy; John 10:10.

***

After watching my mother fight so hard for true love, only to have it ripped away from her; I thought my life would be the same. I thought to myself, how could I ever be at peace or have what she couldn't have? How could my life be so grand when she'd dealt with so much heartache? How could God bless me when my family was struggling?

You see, the real issue was that I knew I was chosen. But it had been a thorn in my side for many years. So, each time I laid with a man or woman it was only because of fear. Running was easier than facing who God said I was. Yet, amid all my hesitations, he still called me his own.

He whispered to me that I was renewed and that he would restore all of time I spent making bad decisions. I know that there are many spaces in between my story; and there is a reason for that. Since, this will be a long series, I decided to do an overview in book one. This is one of those cases where you can read-between-the-lines. It also gives you the room to reflect on your own story. Many things held me back from coming forward and I wonder what words you may have to reveal. I implore you to do it scared; do it unsure, do it with just a little faith because in the end your words will still matter. It is up to you how much you share, but the enemy wins if you stay completely silent. He never wanted me to reveal that I slept with women, battled with pornography, caught sexual transmitted diseases, suffered from daddy issues as well as mommy issues and found myself on the verge of suicide. He knew that if he could keep me silent then I would not heal. If you recall in my dedication, I urged you to ask yourself these two questions:

1. *What is at the root of my despair?* Your answer may be many things or just one. For me, it was abandonment and rejection. The cycle started with my mother choosing her party life over us and my father not being there at all. Then, it continued when I lost my virginity. I was expecting my partner and my parents to complete me. But only my heavenly father could do that. The love of Christ is what I had been searching for all along.

2. *What things are triggering for me?*

My biggest trigger was rejection and the fear of loss. When I started my healing journey, I learned that I self-sabotaged things because I feared they would end badly. I lived my life as if failure was at the end of the journey, so I wanted to get life before life got me. On the same note, having things work out and be successful also scared me. If I believed in something good, then I had to maintain hope; and that was not an option for me. A hopeless life sounded better than having faith only to be let down. This tug of war went against the word of God because his word stands on faith.

*Download the Reveal to Heal Clarity Workbook from **www.delisatreshelle.com/shop**

***

Hebrews 11:1

Now faith is confidence in what we hope for and assurance about what we do not see.

Regardless, of the outcome, I could never lose by trusting in God. He will make your crooked paths straight and give you the true desires of your heart once you submit.

Matthew 6: 33

But seek first his kingdom and his righteousness, and all these things will be given to you as well.

My mama had been married for about three years and we were attending an apostolic church. But I could not get into the vibe like everyone else; I barely sang or opened my mouth to worship. A part of me was nervous because I didn't like anyone looking at me doing anything. While the other part had been blocked by the enemy. There was a supernatural force that kept my mouth bound. As if a muzzle was placed over it, preventing me from speaking. So, even if I wanted to release the words, I couldn't.

It had taken a while for me to get acquainted with my stepdad. Things were rapidly changing, and I'd grown accustomed to our lives before him. For a couple of years, we had finally seen our mother single; at least partially. Though my stepdad didn't deserve my disrespect, I still acted out. Mainly because I didn't like the way my mama let him come in and have control over our household. But of course, I did not know anything about marriage. I was just ready to get out of my mama's house and start my own life. I'd spent so many years longing for things that were beyond my reach.

***

While I was on the verge of a teenage breakdown, my sexuality was reawakened. In a way it had never been before. With cell phones becoming more advanced, it was easy to search for things on the internet. So, in my quest for answers, I found myself being pulled back into pornography and it sparked a new desire for sex. But even with my desire, being intimate still felt odd to me. In my mind, watching the videos was better because I was not actually doing it with anyone. However, pornography isolated me, and it made me feel worse because my need for masturbation grew. I felt unclean and impure, but I could not bring myself to stop. A flame had been ignited and it would lead to a pornography addiction for many years to come.

I was almost a High School graduate and still a virgin. Though, I'd had an experience with a girl. What happened in my childhood was not a reflection of how I saw my future. I struggled to understand what had happened to my dreams of waiting for marriage to have sex. But that is what happens when the roots of a thing are left to rot without acknowledgement or a plan for restoration.

We only had about a month left before graduation and everything was inviting me in. So, I started to pick up, mimic, and subconsciously adapt to what was going on around me. The encounter I'd had with the other girl led to a new side of promiscuity.

I wanted to dress sexier like the women on television. They wore heels that accentuated their legs, and their hair was always done up with extensions. So, I desired to be just like them, and my first job gave me the opportunity to buy new things. The closer I got to becoming an adult, the more I wanted to be one. I rebelled against my mama and my attitude changed. I wasn't the timid little girl anymore. At least, not on the outside. My previous wardrobe was created around my old personality; bland and unrevealing. So, I exchanged my faded Abercrombie jeans and Hollister shirts for tank tops, sexy dresses, shorter shorts, and other exposing pieces of clothing. The sexier I dressed the more I felt a pull to have sex. As soon as I changed my style, boys and men started to act differently towards me; and I was not used to that type of attention. I'd gotten used to being on the outside of the crowd. Everything I'd done before was never enough. The popular group had their picks' and for the longest time, I was not a part of the inner circle. Until I camouflaged myself. The change in my wardrobe caused me to get just as much attention as the other girls. But I still longed to be seen beyond my skimpy pieces of clothing.

***

The Church had become a big part of our lives. We attended with people from various neighborhoods within our city. I didn't notice it at first but overtime I'd started to make a connection with a guy around my age from another side of town. He was much different than the guys I talked to previously on the phone. He had a maturity and honesty about him that was intriguing. It seemed like he saw straight through me, and it was the kind of observation I'd been hoping to receive all along. I could not fool him or be dishonest with him and I liked that about our friendship. I had grown tired of faking it and it felt good to be open and vulnerable. Several months later, our friendship turned into something more. Call it a High School Sweetheart or just plain old young love; but whatever it was, it felt real. Crazy right? I was only months away from my eighteenth birthday and things were finally shifting for me.

He was so unlike me. Even at a young age, he had a love and understanding for Christ that was beyond our years. His boldness and confidence in God continued to pull me in. I admired that about him. In church, he praised and worshipped in a way I never could. It made me want to come out of my shell even more. It also made me want to be a better person. I felt sexy with him but in an innocent way. I felt loved. I shared things with him that were secrets to the other people in my life. We laughed, often, and it nurtured my soul; and because of his relationship with God, I found myself wanting to know Christ for myself. He loved Church so I wanted to love it too. However, that didn't last long.

Though some of our conversations started to venture towards sex I still was not ready to take it to the next level. I'd already slipped up with the girl and kissed a couple of boys, but I wanted things with him to be pure. However, the relationship I had with my mother was very strained and some of the things she said cut me to the core. They may have been simple words to someone else, but for me it seemed like I couldn't do anything right in her eyes. Everything I did was judged and placed under a microscope; picked apart. I was accused of being a fast girl, when I was battling with sexual confusion, the fear of homosexuality, and an overall lack of understanding. Everyone knew I was still a virgin, but she was the only one who acted like I wasn't. I don't believe she realized the weight of her words or accusations. It may have been a way to scare me into not doing it. But I was still traumatized. I still felt beaten down and lonely.

***

My mother is not to blame for the decision I made but I cannot deny her influence in it. One day I woke up and everything inside of me snapped. I'd spent so many years trying to be perfect and it all came crashing down on me. So, I convinced myself that I should no longer care about doing the right things. The conversations with my boyfriend were spicier and more X-rated. He really wanted to have sex and I started to give it some serious consideration. I figured if my mother was already accusing me of doing it, then it wouldn't make a bit of difference to act it out.

The horrible sex stories I heard from the girls at school played in the back of my mind, but I pushed them aside. During some of our pow wow sessions I shuttered at their mention of their first times being painful and degrading. There were girls who were left alone on cold floors after giving their bodies away while others were disrespected days later. I didn't think my story would end that way. At very least, I had waited until I found love. In my mind, my boyfriend was my soulmate. Although, those girls may have thought the same thing. We all probably fell under the assumption that we would be with our mate beyond High School and College.

As the weeks went on my plan to lose my virginity was set in motion. I had no idea how we would do it, but we found a way. My best friend at the time had her own car so she was the driver. After ensuring my boyfriend's room was safe and secure, the door closed on my dreams and my purity.

Though my first time was unlike the girls I heard stories from, it was still frightening. I was not left on a floor, disrespected, or filled with pain. In fact, there was not much discomfort at all. It was a pleasant experience psychically but a detrimental one spiritually. I was unaware of the spirit realm. I had no idea that I was opening a demonic portal that would follow me into adulthood.

***

1 Corinthians 6:18

Flee from sexual immorality. All other sins a person commits are outside the body, but whoever sins sexually, sins against their own body.

***

Because I lacked knowledge on how much intimacy before marriage damages you, I followed my flesh. My relationship had turned into lots of I Love You's, plans for the future, and sex.

I never told my mother about my first time, but I think she knew. I was too nervous, scared, and embarrassed to say anything, but my best friend had revealed my secret. I was hurt but most of all I couldn't grasp why she did that; especially when I specifically asked her not to. I'm sure she had her own reasons, but it was the first time I felt the sting of betrayal.

Just like I had my own reasons for not telling my mama; I wanted to have more time and tell her when I was ready. But I also did not want her to be right. She could have flown off the handle and caused more damage to our fragile relationship. So, it was a personal choice to remain silent.

6

After my first time

Blog Post: June 5, 2019

TRUE LOVE WILL BE COMPLETE, LACKING NOTHING. It won't be easily angered but instead kind, patient, and unconditional. You will receive the kind of love that is based on who you are, not what you do. You won't have to be put together and primped every second of the day. This kind of love won't blame you for your shortcomings but instead embrace your flaws as a unique part of you. True love won't be destructive nor hold your past against you. It won't use your faults as an excuse to tear you down. How do I get to this type of love? You may ask. The first step is learning to love yourself. We hear that all the time, but most people are still walking around expecting someone else to fix what they won't fix within themselves. What is love in its purest form? The answer is quite simple. God's love is the purest you will ever find. Once you accept that as truth it will be easier to decline what you do not deserve. No one taught me what love really was. And maybe like me, you had to bear witness to emotional and sometimes physical abuse which distorted your view of the word. You may also lack the knowledge of it because of what you personally experienced in life. Those encounters can make you feel like you are underserving of love. But you are. I know we don't see pure love that often. But what if I told you that all you desire is standing on the other side of fear? Fear of the unknown. Fear stops us from demanding more. We don't want to start over with someone else, so we keep ourselves bound to an unhealthy attachment. What I do know is that Christ loves you; and there is nothing you can hide from him. He sees all and knows all. Yet, he accepts you today and he will forevermore. Regardless of where you are in your life right now, nothing is too much for him. I encourage you to take your focus away from others and embrace yourself. All of you. One scar. One wound, at a time.

Shreveport, La 2007

My second sting of betrayal was only months after the first one. Sex changed everything. It made me hypersensitive and emotional for no reason. However, I was not overexaggerating at the pain I felt when I found out my boyfriend had been talking to another girl. I didn't think I would ever survive the heartbreak and facing it was all too much. We had broken up and I just wanted to feel again. So, I explored and did what I wanted. Consequences were far from my mind as I gave my body to another man. However, I was falling headfirst into the enemy's traps unaware. I thought having other encounters would make me feel better, but my heart was too weak.

Yet, it didn't take long for my initial escapades to come to an end, and I found myself right back in the arms of my ex-boyfriend. Our second wave of encounters were much deeper than the first ones.

So much had happened during our time apart and us reconnecting was even more chaotic. We quarreled over the smallest things and there was more hurt than love. I wish I'd known about self-reflection and healing from trauma after being wounded. But I didn't and reconnecting with him only stifled those wounds.

During it all, I found myself suffocating and my consciousness tugged at me. It was like God sat on one shoulder while the devil sat on the other. The freedom that I once felt was no longer there. I started to really think about what I was doing, and it triggered some conviction. Even though I didn't know what it was at the time because I still did not have a personal relationship with God. But, at the most inconvenient times, scriptures would pop up in my mind or I would not so randomly remember something my grandmother taught us as kids. It made me realize that I was living the kind of life I'd sworn against.

When I felt loved, everything was all good between my ex and me. My intention was to never be with anyone else or be caught up in any mess. It may have been him. It may have been me. But we were not enough for each other anymore. That realization slapped me in the face, and I pushed down the scriptures I heard in my head. I knew I was supposed to change my ways but running was much easier. I believed that participating in more sexual encounters would erase my old memories. With that, my new search began. I would prove to my ex and myself that I could recreate the love we once had. Ironically, right as I began to place those thoughts in my head, the men around me came on stronger. I fed into it because I believed that anything would be better than the situation I'd been tied to. They would not lie to me or cheat on me. They would not make me feel bad or leave me feeling broken. Right?

Wrong. My biggest fears started to manifest. I had nightmares of being heartbroken again and rejected; but that is exactly what happened.

In my pain, I thought of creating another version of myself. One that would not be left in distress. One that would be the head and not the tail. One that would do the hurting and not get hurt. She would be the one to call all the shots. She would live and live well. No other man would ever hurt her. She could hide her wounds and be emotionless; she could be free. My alter ego, Treshelle was born, and she was out for blood.

***

Sex had made me consider another person in my life's plans. It made me want to let someone else inside of my heart. But sex broke me. The plans of getting married to my ex and having children were washed away. I wanted to become a lawyer and attend Spellman in Atlanta. I dreamed of living a grand life away from my hometown. Yet none of that happened. Our disconnection was the last straw to break the camel's back. After realizing that my dreams were not going to come true, I mentally planned my escape. But you can't outrun pain and I took my scars right along with me.

***

My stepdad had been talking to me about the Navy for months. I'd originally halted my plans because my ex. But I finally listened to him about leaving home and joined the armed forces. We had created an unbreakable bond over his naval recollections, and he'd turned out the be the perfect father for me and my brother.

As the weeks went on, I felt lighter because my date of departure was approaching. My mother, stepdad, and I had sat down along with my Navy Recruiter to seal the deal. As the tears rolled down my mother's face, I did not share any of her pain. She was releasing me into the unknown and I am sure it was one of the hardest things she ever had to do but for me it meant a new life. One away from all the things and people who had hurt me. At eighteen years old, I left my hometown of Shreveport, Louisiana in the cool of November as Great Lakes, Illinois awaited my arrival.

A Letter to the Brokenhearted Wo(man)

Wo(man), you are enough to be loved. All those dreams you had as a little girl or boy can still come true if you just believe. I know it seems like so many other women have something that you don't possess. They appear to have the perfect life with their families, and you find yourself wondering when that will happen for you. You may see people stepping out on faith to start their business, write their book, speak at conferences, and so on, while you feel trapped. At night you deal with a broken heart and tears flow down your face with no one around to help you wipe them. You too feel unseen. But I see you. You may have spent your life trying to protect those around you from your own brokenness. You are the strong one. The one that everyone expects to have it all together because they either don't know or don't care about the battles you face internally. The invisible mask that covers your lips keeps your true words hidden. I was that woman. The one who wanted to see everyone else happy. The one who tried to take care of everyone else first. I used to believe that God would get to me when it was my time to step out, but he had been waiting on me the entire time. So, that tells me he has been waiting on you too. I dare you to be bold and brave. I dare you to dream. I dare you to heal and shed the pieces of yourself that no longer serve you, because your destiny awaits.

PART THREE

Joining
The
Armed Forces

7

A Girl Running

To Mama: December 17, 2018

Mother, I love you dearly. I never thought about the times your heart broke because your own dreams went up into flames. You had to watch them be burned away and your aspirations turned into something else. A desire to do anything you could for your children. Strength and dedication arose, and you carried us on your back. In your own way, you tried to put us before anything else. My brother and I became your dreams. No, you weren't perfect, no one is, but you tried.

I couldn't understand it at first because my own bitterness caused me to ignore the pain behind your eyes. How scared you must have been, at nineteen years old? Your entire life ahead of you. The start of your life. So, I believe that you were just exploring and trying to find yourself amid your own pain. Maybe, you were running too. I used to watch you put black eyeliner under your eyes and it was something I could not wait to do once I got older. I wanted to dress like you because I admired your style. I dreamed of being as pretty and as confident as you. But, I wonder, what you must have been hiding to protect us. We've spent so many years with different pieces of our hearts crushed. You wanted a daughter that was your best friend. I wanted to be noticed and feel loved. I believe we both played movie scenes out in our heads, but we could not put the actions behind our scenarios. Our intentions fell short but thank God there is still time for restoration. I am here because of you and your dreams still await. It is not too late, in fact, I believe that you will arrive at your destination just in time.

Shreveport, La November 2007

I strutted across Shreveport Regional Airport with my bags and family in tow. I tried to take mental pictures of their faces, their laughter, and the way we all meshed as I awaited my flight. They stayed until the very last minute, watching me enter the gate of which my plane would leave.

As I walked into the airplane corridor, I didn't know what to expect in the weeks to come. I'd never flown before, but it wasn't as scary as I thought it would be. Instead, my blood warmed with enthusiasm. I made small talk with a few other recruits that were headed to the same place. One girl was nervous, so I removed my headphones and talked to her.

The plane drifted up and into the clouds as I watched from my window seat. God sent his angels to encamp around me because even then I felt a sense of protection and peace. After a few hours, we touched down in Illinois. As soon as the air changed, I knew I was far away from home. The entire atmosphere was different. There were large groups of other recruits huddled together as we all waited to be taken into the confines of basic training. I don't believe any of us was prepared for our new life.

The cold of November hit me like splinters piercing through my skin. I had never experienced that type of weather. The hairs on my arm stood at attention and pricked me from inside my thin sweater. I was severely underdressed, though, I don't even believe three coats would've been enough. White clouds of air billowed from my mouth and my stiff joints turned into frostbite. The coldness along with the butterflies in my stomach put me on high alert. Everything startled me. From the weather to the sound of the petty officers screaming at us to form cohesive lines. It all sparked flames of regret. The previous joy and curiosity I had was overshadowed by the thought of, what am I doing? I'd spent the weeks before my departure from Shreveport whipping myself into shape; or so I thought. But once I stepped onto the streets of Recruit Training Command at Naval Station Great Lakes, I realized that I had bitten off more than I could chew.

My division was split up between males and females. The males slept separately across the hall. Once the female recruits settled in on our side, we were each given a bunk mate. The RPO (Recruit Petty Officer) called out our last names only, along with our rack number and we scattered across the gray floor to our appropriate spaces. My bunk was on the top and though it was noted as the best space to have, it did not help me. I was always the last one to arrive on the line at reveille.

Our first two weeks moved like molasses and in the slowness of time, I seriously wanted to grow closer to God. Especially after finding out someone had given me an std. It was the first time I realized that your actions would follow you regardless of where you were. The Doctor looked at me like I had two heads. I am sure he was so used to curing sexual transmitted diseases that he didn't understand my confusion. I saw in the chair hyperventilating, an innocent age of eighteen. I really believed that my life had taken the worse turn ever. And what bothered me the most was the fact that I had gone so long without even knowing I had it. There were so many parts of me that were in denial. I refused to acknowledge that I had been so reckless, and I went over in my head a million times trying to figure out where it had come from. I could not blame my ex when I had been with other men. The news just made me sick to my stomach and from that point on, I started to hate men. At least black men. There was a point where I decided that I would just date outside of my race. Because those who looked like me had hurt me way too bad. Before I made it to my first command, I already knew that I was done with my own race. At least that is what I thought. Until brokenness yet again caused me to do unthinkable things. Boot camp was one of the challenging times in my life and with that my need for something bigger sprang up in a heightened awareness. Though, I still didn't know much about having a relationship with God, I started to pray. More than I had in my entire life. Each day I woke up and asked him to deliver me from all the distress I was going through. Of course, we call on Jesus when we are in trouble. But God didn't come to my rescue, even though I know he was still there. Some things you must go through and not around. There was no way the Navy was sending me home, regardless of how bad I wanted to leave;

I couldn't, and I started to realize that there was a purpose behind God's plans. **Ironically the very place that I ran away from was the place I wanted to run back to.**

Other than talking to God I spent most of my time writing letters home. It was the one thing we could do, and I took advantage of the opportunity. I sent several apologizing to my mama and stepdad for my rebellion in High School: along with letters of comfort to my grandmother. I had gotten the new life I wanted but it was not the one I had in mind.

Great Lakes, Illinois December 2007

"Sound off. One two. Sound off. Three four. Sound off one, two, three, four." I was one month into my new life and cadence had become a part of my everyday routine. I continued my

conversations with God and had found some sense of faith. It gave me strength and that was what I needed to make it through each day.

My time away allowed for hours of reflection. I realized that I lacked grace towards my family, my ex, and my city in general. There was a bitterness I carried but I was not ready to forgive or let go of the pain. I'd grown so accustomed to pushing feelings down and pretending that I wasn't bothered that God could never heal me properly. I knew I was hurting but I just refused to let it stop me. Though, it should have. So many times, over the years, the pain should have made me stop. Had I stopped, I would've been pruned much sooner and would've probably produced more good fruit than bad. However, the latter became my life. I held on more to my childhood scars than anything else. The Navy allowed me the opportunity to camouflage myself and becoming someone that the rest of the world didn't know. I could be whoever I wanted to be and that is exactly what I did. Way before the pandemic ever occurred, I'd worn a mask years before. An invisible one. The kind that kept my real secrets, fears, and insecurities hidden.

Poem: Running Away

Written February 6. 2018

You stood there in a different
city...
Hair astray, wild but not free.
New faces flash before your eyes.
You smile.
Yet, the bricks weigh heavier than
they did last time.
This new place should feel like
home;
But you're still running away.
Be still.
What you seek is not in this
scenery either;
It's inside of you ...

8

A Girl Injured

Great Lakes, Illinois December 2007

WOKE UP ON DECEMBER 19, 2007 to the screaming voice of my RPO just like any other day in basic training. But that morning at reveille was different. I tried to move but I felt arrested. My legs refused to move; it was like a ton of bricks lay on top of the left one. Being on the top rack, I had to use a climb down method to get on the floor. Normally, I would jump down but when I looked at my legs to see what was going on I could not believe my eyes. They widened in horror and stuck out of my head like saucers. Upon inspection, I saw that my entire left leg was completely swollen. From my feet to the middle of my thighs and not just minor swelling. I had never seen anything so abnormal looking. My leg looked deformed. I whispered to the recruit I had gotten close to over the previous weeks so she could look too. We tried to sneak into the head (restroom), but we were caught before we could make it inside of the doors. Our RPO was yelling again but this time it was directly at us. We were so caught up in trying to see my leg that we didn't see our entire division already standing at parade rest. My attitude had become very bad in basic training and that day was no different. So, as our person in charge barked out orders, I quickly let her know what was going on. But, after revealing to her what my friend and I had been looking at, I started to feel ashamed. We slept in PT (physical training) shorts and my entire leg was on display for everyone to mock.

The entire rank had been broken because she had no choice but to stop and listen to what I was saying. In the background, girls whispered in shock as they noticed my leg too. My leg was literally four times its normal size. The RPO wasn't happy of course because my situation caused everything to be shifted *out of order*.

I recounted what I knew had happened. Letting her know that the day before, while we were running, I felt my leg twist and it was followed by a sharp pain. With that, she begrudgingly sent me to see Medical.

Once I trampled over to see the doctor, retelling my story once again, I believed that I would be sent home. He agreed that I had sprung something, but I was not sent home. I was only given a light limited duty (LLD) chit for three days and sent back to my division. I had to be limited in participating with the group for the physical part of our training. I never received an official diagnosis. There was no recovery plan drafted up for me. I was just told to elevate my leg at night and after those three days, I was released back into my division and marked fit for full duty. My leg was still swollen but after my initial chit it was ignored. So, I dealt with it because I did not have a choice. There were only a few weeks left in basic training and I would soon be graduating. Mentally, I was determined to push through the pain. But I could not. Not only did I miss graduating with my division. I was set back for an extra two months because of my disability. When it came time to tell my family about my leg, I was a little hesitant because I did not want them worrying even more. But I finally wrote a letter to my mom and let her know what was going on. She thought she could just call the Recruit Training Command and complain to get me sent home but that is not how things worked. I was not eligible to be released from boot camp. In the middle of everything going on around me, I prayed for it all to be *over.*

9

The First Time God Saved the Girl

Shreveport, La 1996

The little girl inside my head taunted me again. She sat in front of me and refused to move. This time she was in the mirror. Each time I looked in the mirror, through her eyes one word came to mind. *Abandon.* No one sees me or understands me. I'm overlooked. I don't exist. The things she told me, I believed because no one said otherwise. Amid family and while in my grandmother's presence, I still felt alone.

Joshua 1:9 King James version

Have not I commanded thee? Be strong and of a good courage; be not afraid, neither be thou dismayed: for the LORD thy God is with thee whithersoever thou goest.

Shreveport, La 2020

I was scared to do it God's way. He'd given me visions of how things would turn out, but I couldn't accept what he'd told me. Fear of the unknown drove the wheel of my car for six hours into a place I'd just come from just years before.

The man wasn't the same by any means. I refused to believe that I was who God said I was. My desire for a mate came rushing back after being single for three years. I'd gotten used to the fact that I was celibate and waiting on God. Then something happened. I took what I believed God said and ran with it. I tried to make it happen in my own timing because the desire to be married had gotten so strong.

The closer I got to being whole the more I wanted a companion. I had to realize that the enemy didn't want me to be healed. Nor did the *internal me*. Becoming whole was a foreign thing because I'd lived in brokenness for so long. How did I get here? It's been a week since I left my place of comfort and there is nowhere to run anymore. As I rode down the streets of this city, my hometown; my eyes lit up in wonder. Out of the corner of my eye I caught a glimpse of a dead-end sign and the Holy Spirit rushed over me. He said that to move forward I had to first go back. What would my life be like if I truly laid bare before Christ and let him all the way in?

Genesis 37:24 English Standard Version

And they took him and threw him into a pit. The pit was empty; there was no water in it.

God allowed Joseph to be thrown into the pit because he needed him to go through a **process** *before* **the promise.** Joseph's dreams would indeed come true but not before he became persecuted. God spoke to me so clearly and said that I had to be *processed first.* Before

I become one with a man, I must first become one with him. The little girl inside me has finally sat still long enough for me to receive God in his way, his timing, and his process.

Great Lakes, Illinois February 2008

My feet hovered over the edge of the diving platform. The navy officers only gave us half a breath before pushing us in. My arms crossed over my chest in anticipation and horror. My tiny frame quivered from the cold room and the fritters in my belly halted me in place. I was determined to make it through. Injury had already kept me from graduating with my division. The swimming came in third place. Second place lay the fear of succeeding. Yes, I feared passing. Afraid of what my life would be outside of basic training. The first time I jumped, a long-life hook came out of nowhere to pull me up. I was drowning. The world went black, but it was peaceful. My ears filled with water and in all the chaos I felt the hand of God upon my life. In my drowning moment I faintly heard the yelling from a man telling me to grab the stick. I was lifted out of the pool and my disappointed heart carried me back to the locker room to get dressed. After that, I had to train more. The kiddy pool is what they called it there. It was where the not-so-great swimmers learned just enough to pass the swim test. So, I went back to square one. I trained some more and learned how to swim the way that was easiest for me, on my back. It didn't matter how you learned; you just had to grasp the lesson. I remember looking at the other recruits making the long swim and wondered how they did it. What pushed them to pass? Not the ones who were experts but the ones who were in the same beginner's pool as me but had made it to the finish line.

The second time, I made it about 35 yards into the 50-yard swim. That time, I was stronger and more determined. Still disappointed that I didn't make it all the way, I went into my berthing with a little more hope. My perspective changed and because I was so close, I wanted to succeed. So, I was back, in the same place I'd been two times before. It was my third time making the deep-water jump. Unlike the other times, I listened to God. I heard him tell me that I could do it. I told myself that my family needed to see me again and vice versa. I made up my mind that my life wouldn't end in Illinois. I would cry, fight, scrape, and crawl if I had to. With that mindset, I made the deep-water jump, on my own. I didn't wait for the officers to push me in, I jumped on my own. I swam, on my back, nonstop until I knew I would pass. I could hear the men and women around me cheering me on, their voices showing excitement and a little mockery. They knew I'd been stuck in that swim test. They saw me fail. They saw me learning to flow with the water. But in the end, they saw me win. Once my hand found the other side, I gripped the concrete and rose from the water.

My swim story is much like my relationship with Christ. I've failed so many times. There were times when I lost hope and thought it was over. Times when I felt the water covering my ears and felt my body weighed down by the currency. But just like the life hook, he reached in and saved me. He pleaded with me to grip his hand

and release all my fears. The test was never ending and most of the time it took me losing to learn the lesson; and eventually pass.

***

Sometimes you must *go back* to *move forward*. The lesson from my swim test and my arrival back to my hometown is that I was not quite prepared to move ahead because I needed more training to pass the tests. Therefore, I believe that's why God would only let me go so far before pulling me right back. It can be frustrating to stop especially when you're so used to moving swiftly. However, slowing down was the best thing I could've done in my life. Social Media, pressure from friends and family, your own goals and such can make you feel like you must compete. But what are you competing with if you are still broken? Don't get me wrong, healing is an evolutionary journey, so each season requires more digging, but if you have never even started, how do you expect God to give you the desires of your heart? Before you can do anything else, give God your yes. To whatever you know he is telling you to do. Whether that is forgiving someone, revisiting your past to understand your own trauma areas, starting a blog, writing a book, embarking on a business, leaving a relationship, or beginning one, quitting or starting a job, going to school; whatever it is, DO IT. Because you won't have true peace until you do. We can find glory in God's wholeness, knowing that he is willing and available to deal with all our broken pieces. Nothing is too hard for him, and you can trust him with your *hidden things*. I had to first go to God in secret before I could finish this book. Though, my process is not over, I believe that the journey ahead is one filled with love, joy, and God's glorious plan for my life.

***

Hebrews 1:3

The Son is the radiance of God's glory and the exact representation of his being, sustaining all things by his powerful word. After he had provided purification for sins, he sat down at the right hand of the Majesty in heaven.

Journal Entry September 17, 2021

On yesterday my heart was extremely heavy. Have you ever felt like everything was hitting you at one time? I am currently in that space. I don't understand God's next move and because of this I have chased my own tail for months. I fought with God to just leave me alone because I wanted a normal life, like everyone else. But the closure I needed was not with another person, place, or thing. It was with God. Three years ago, I started to mentally push away from him before it ever happened physically. At the time, he was asking me to trust him with my heart and I couldn't do that. I could trust him with most things, but my heart was off limits. It had been broken too many times and too many uncertainties were buried deep within. My insecurities told me I was not qualified enough to be chosen. Yet, God handpicked me.

***

2 Thessalonians 2:14

To this end he handpicked you for salvation through the gospel so that you would have the glory of our Lord Jesus Christ. The Passion Translation.

***

In my prayer time this morning I simply told God, "I am tired." It was then that he urged me to speak out loud the question that had been sitting heavy on my chest. So, in my secret place I whispered through tears, "God, where is my help?"

The words were barely audible but the minute they were released from my lips, there was a shift in the atmosphere.

Angels entered my room, and it was then that God told me to move. My steps were ordained by Christ himself and the minute I reached my destination, the room was already set and prepared for me. So, I pose this question to you. Who, what, or where are you running from?

Epilogue

An Entry from my Journal: August 24. 2021

I am starting to find a pattern in my life, writing, and overall history of self-exploration in general. My struggles are almost always linked to disobedience. God would tell me something, I would struggle with what he said and then I would disobey. I believe this is deep-rooted in childhood trauma. Somewhere, somehow, I decided that I would become a rebel. I believe it was around the time I truly realized that my father was not coming for me. There was no saviour. No one to come and pick me up and help me put my pieces back together. But I was deceived. God had been there the entire time. Watching me and loving me. The seeds of rejection and abandonment were planted early. I always felt alone and unseen, rejected, and misunderstood. Nothing was ever good enough. I remember being laughed at a lot in my family and at school. They said many different things but one memory that sticks is someone saying, "You can't ever do anything right." I would also hear things like "You are always messing everything up." I was the last one to catch on to the joke, the last one to understand what was going on in the room. If I was supposed to play along, I always failed because my head was elsewhere. More than likely in some sort of fantasy or foreign place where I could escape my own reality. Overtime because I believed I could never do anything right. I didn't do anything right. I started to rebel and do things I wanted. I was first disobedient to my mother and just authority in general. I hated being told what to do or how to do it. I wanted to do it my way or it was the highway. This carried on for many years and is something I still struggle with today. Because of the seeds, the enemy planted in my ear by people closest to me, and peers at school I rejected doing the right thing. I was sneaky and conniving. Manipulative and selfish. Since I was hurt and felt pain then I only cared about myself. I have seen these same habits show up in my adult life. Lying to get away with something because I was afraid of what the truth may bring. Deep down I wanted to do the right thing, but it felt like I couldn't. Like something was preventing me from doing what I knew I was supposed to do. Now, at 31 years of age, I still struggle with obedience. This time what started with parents and teachers has drifted towards my relationship with God. Because I didn't feel like I could trust those around me, I didn't listen. It is the same way. Now, I am trying to pick up all the pieces I have lost or abandoned over the years. Pieces of myself. Histories and memories that I pressed down because they were too hard to deal with. I now know that I wasn't fighting with my mom. I wasn't fighting with the bullies at school or my teachers. I was internally fighting against the unseen spiritual principalities that were sent to destroy me so that I may never walk in my destiny. My suicide encounter came later but the seeds of not feeling enough, ugly, unwanted, and unseen started long before I ever sat in my car with a bottle of pills in my hands. It started when

I was around five.

***

I believe that last journal entry summarized Childhood Scars. As you can tell from reading a portion of my story, I ran in circles before coming to a stop. Because life had broken me down so many times, I never allowed God the opportunity to fully heal me from within. Revealing my wounds scared me. Peeling back layers of regret and unforgiveness scared me. I never wanted to revisit my childhood. But I couldn't move forward without doing so. You may find that some of your decisions and actions are based on those fading memories from years ago. Like me, you may have allowed the words of others to determine how you lived your life. But right now, you can acknowledge that and make a turn. No longer shall you carry what others have done to you. Put it down! Do not continue to make bad choices because you are hurting. The best way to get back what belongs to you is to live a peaceful life while walking in purpose and staying in obedience to God. You may not know how to do that. I refuse to tell you that following Christ is easy, but it is the best thing I have ever done. No one could fix me or heal my broken places. It was only the love of God that was able to cover all my iniquities.

So, if you are struggling to make sense of your purpose, I implore you to sit. Take a moment and remove the facade. I know things around you may look ugly. You may feel trapped and all you want is for someone to notice your pain; to give you a hug and allow you time to find comfort in their grip. But, let me be the first one to embrace you, through my words, because I do see you. And I want you to know that even if it does not look like it right now, everything is okay. God will finish the work he started in you, and it will be beyond your greatest expectations.

***

James 1:4 King James Version

But let patience have her perfect work, that ye may be perfect and entire, wanting nothing.

8 Messages to my younger self.

Number One: Move

It is okay to start over. God has been pulling you in a different direction for a while now and you have been afraid, but God is waiting on you to take the first step.

Number Two: Trust Your Gut

You struggle with making the right choices. This is because you always want things to be perfect and the thought of making the wrong choice keeps you at a standstill. However, overthinking is the very thing that leads you into the bad choices you try so hard to avoid. Trust your gut (Holy Spirit) and let that be your guide.

Number Three: Finish Your Manuscript

There has been a story brewing on the inside of you for some time now. God has given you many manuscripts to write but you overanalyze the words he wants you to write. The key is to just start. Do not run this time. Sit in his presence and allow him to cultivate you. Allow his voice in and the words you need will start to pour out of you.

Number Four: Your Anointing Isn't a Mistake

You feel as if your calling is a burden. The weight is so pertinent that you tend to give up often because you are trying to carry it by yourself. But it wasn't created just for your hands. It was meant to be guided by the Holy Spirit. Anytime you try to go alone you will face unnecessary hardships. But once you place your life and calling in God's grip, everything will become easier to carry. Your anointing was never a mistake. God didn't make the wrong choice when he chose you. He knew exactly what he was doing.

Number Five: Forgive Your Father

Your father grew up in a completely different time than you. Things were not black and white for him. The way he was taught. The things he saw. The people he was around. All of that shaped him into the person he became. But he never wanted to be that way. He wanted to be there but in his own mind he couldn't. It isn't an excuse; it is just a reality. Your father fell short. It is time to forgive him. Not for him but for you.

Number Six: Forgive Your Mother

Forgive your mother. You only get one and while she is still here, love on her. Honor her. Show her you care and that you aren't holding on to things for the sake of holding on.

Number Seven: Let God Lead the Way.

Follow. Those are the only instructions. Follow. Do not lead. Do not try to walk ahead of God. Do not try to create your own path. Simply follow and obey.

Number Eight: Think & Speak Goodness.

John 10:10 says that the enemy came to steal, kill, and destroy but Christ came to give life more abundantly. Your mind has been all over the place. To and FRO. The enemy loves to play tricks on you because he knows that your lack of faith and disbelief in some areas causes you to doubt God. The best way to combat this is to Think & Speak Goodness. Start with one thought. One change of heart. One scripture. One day at a time.

A Message from Christ

I will walk beside you every step of the way. Trust that my partner, The Holy Spirit, is always nearby. As you seek the part of you that is buried underneath the muck, you will discover that Hidden Treasures lie in the places you have yet to uncover.

Acknowledgments

I would first like to give honor to Christ, my savior, and redeemer. Your love saved me. And to my family and friends, I love you dearly.

Other Books by Leaked from My Pen

Rekindled: Hidden Treasures:

Forgiving my Incarcerated Father

www.delisatreshelle.com/shop

Unapologetically: I am a Man

https://amzn.to/3zt7Xmu

The concepts behind these poems are designed to see, feel, and despise the pain of slavery, and injustices created since the inception of America.

About The Author

DeLisa Treshelle is an author, inspirational speaker, manuscript delivery coach, and prophetic artist. She is a Shreveport native and owner of Leaked from My Pen, LLC; a book writing company that helps aspiring authors write and self-publish their God-given book idea. DeLisa is also the creator of Ordained Canvas, an art company where she creates personalized prophetic art pieces. Her goal is to provide Mental & Emotional therapy to others using writing & art. DeLisa's podcast Uncovered Through Christ is available now on Apple Podcast. Her book entitled Childhood Scars is the first release from her memoir series Uncovered Through Christ and you can find it on

Amazon.com. DeLisa helps broken-hearted men and women recover from past traumas and walk in restoration.

DeLisa's Contact Info:

Email: author@delisatreshelle.com
Website: www.delisatreshelle.com
Instagram: www.instagram.com/delisatwrites
Twitter: www.twitter.com/delisatreshelle
LinkedIn: www.linkedin.com/in/delisatbrown/

Made to Art

House of Treshelle

PROPHETIC ART

Uncovered Through Christ is a Podcast based on the book series by DeLisa Treshelle. Write it down, even if it hurts and allow God the opportunity to heal your broken places. Do you feel as if you are a prophetic scribe? Tune in each week to get clarity along with tips and tools to write your own story.

1 Peter 2:9

But you are a chosen people, a royal priesthood, a holy nation, God's special possession, that you may declare the praises of him who called you

out of darkness into his wonderful light.

Search for Uncovered Through Christ on Apple Podcast!

DeLisa Treshelle

words matter

UNCOVERED

Through Christ

SALVATION

Prayer

At the end of each book, I will be leaving a prayer for salvation. You may ponder on this and even if you aren't prepared now; feel free to come back. Being baptized at a young age did not satisfy my curiosity for Jesus because I had no sense of belief. So, if you want to say this prayer it must first be activated by faith. As demonstrated in my story, there were many things I fell into before even facing God at all. Though, we still have many books to get through just know I would not be writing anything if it were not for the love of Christ. There may be a tug within you, a pull to turn back to your Creator. Do not ignore it because that means God is trying to get your attention. Think on it if you must but ask yourself this question; What would I be losing by trusting and believing in Christ? Proceed to the prayer when you are ready.

***

"I, (state your name), accept Jesus Christ into my heart. I believe that Jesus came to die on the Cross for my sins and that He rose on the seventh day. I repent of all my sins, knowingly

and unknowingly. I ask God to send his angels out to protect me and my family. Please forgive me for any grievances I may have caused you. Take control of my heart and teach me to walk in your ways. I pray by faith that your word is true. By the power of the Holy Spirit, I can do all things through Christ which strengthens me. In Jesus' name, Amen. ``

Visit this link for a follow up.

https://nnye0jgz3te.typeform.com/to/G7RXOLVX

***

Or send an email to

leakedfrommypen@gmail.com

In the subject line put

"Follow up to Salvation Prayer"

Stay Tuned for Book Two: A Woman Redeemed.

Coming Soon!

Made in the USA
Columbia, SC
22 December 2021

51128262R00114